Pass

Contents	Page

written by Susan Hughes

What is salt?

Salt is a mineral
made of sodium and
chloride. It is one of
the most common
minerals in the world.
That's good, because
it is very important
to humans. Why? All
living creatures need
salt to survive.
Think of something
salty. Now imagine
tasting it. Your
tongue has special
taste buds for basic
human tastes such as
sweet, salty, sour and
bitter. The taste buds
for salt are on each
side of the tongue.

Where is salt?

Most of the salt in the world is found in seawater. It is also found in salt lakes and salt springs – and in the earth itself. Scientists believe that oceans once covered a large part of the globe. Then the climate changed, and the oceans dried up in places. Salt was left behind.

Searching for salt

People have always needed salt to survive. In ancient times, people mostly ate meat. But about 10,000 years ago, more and more people began farming. They grew cereals and grains, which have less salt than meat. People needed to add salt to their diet, so they began to search for it.

About 8,000 years ago, people gathered salt from the surface of Xiechi Lake. This is a salt lake in what is now China. About 6,500 years ago, in what is now Azerbaijan, people found rock salt deep in the ground. They created a salt mine that was probably the first one in the world.

Sun + salty water = salt

When people couldn't find salt, they tried to make it. About 5,000 years ago, people in Egypt made salt by using heat from the sun. They created shallow ponds. They let in the seawater, and they waited. Remember: seawater is made of water, salt, and some minerals. Over time, the water evaporated. The salt and minerals were left behind. This kind of salt is called sea salt. The ancient Maya made salt in this way, too.

Fire + salty water = salt

People also made salt using fire. They heated seawater or water from salt springs. The water boiled away. The salt was left behind. Almost 3,000 years ago, in ancient China, people were making salt in this way.

Preserving food

Some foods don't stay fresh for long because bacteria in food can make it go bad. Adding salt to food can slow down the growth of bacteria so it lasts longer. Since ancient times, people have added salt to foods for this reason. For example, in 3,000 BC the Egyptians used salt to preserve meat and fish.

Paying with salt

For a time, salt was so valuable that people used it – instead of gold – to pay for goods! In ancient China, some coins were made of salt. At one time, ancient Roman soldiers were paid with money and some salt. This payment of salt was called a "salarium." The English word "salary" comes from this ancient word "salarium." ("Sal" is the Latin word for salt.)

Salt trade

Everyone has always needed salt, but long ago not everyone could find it or make it. People who did have salt could make some good deals. People without salt were very eager to trade for it, so salt became very valuable. In fact, most early trade routes and roads were made to help people trade salt more easily!

About 6,500 years ago, people in Central Asia were trading salt
for copper and other metals. About 2,500 years ago, people in
Europe also began trading salt. From about 600 to 1,000 AD, salt
was traded for gold in West Africa. Caravans of camels carried the
goods back and forth. One sack of salt was worth one sack of gold!
People fought for control of the salt trade.

Pass the salt please!

Today salt is used in more than 14,000 ways. For example, people use table salt to season food. Table salt is made from rock salt. Workers dig up chunks of rock salt from the ground. They remove other minerals from it, then they put in an additive that prevents the grains of salt from sticking together. They also add iodine because many people around the world don't get enough iodine, which helps protect them from basic health problems.

More uses of salt

Salt is used in many other ways. Some companies make chemicals from salt, then they add chemicals to drinking water and swimming pools to keep them safe. They use them to make thousands of products. Some examples are:

- bleach
- glass
- soap
- plastic
- rubber

Test it!

In countries with severe winter weather, pathways can be icy. Some people put salt on them. Why? This helps to melt the ice. Water with salt in it freezes at lower temperatures than water without salt in it. Test it:

Fill two cups with water. Put two spoonfuls of salt in one. Stir. Put both cups in the freezer. Check how long it takes the water to freeze.

What difference did the salt make?

Salt makes a difference to our lives, too!